FAIRIES 3

Line Art Coloring Book
by Christine Karron

This coloring book is designed for experienced colorists and beginners as well.
Recommended for coloring with markers, colored pencils, pens and/or crayons.
If using wet media place a sheet of thick paper or card stock
behind the coloring page to prevent bleed through.

All illustrations in this book were originally created and traditionally
hand drawn by the artist Christine Karron. For coloring inspirations,
demo videos and more about Christine's artwork visit chkarron.com

No part of this book may be reproduced or transmitted in any form or by any
means, electronic or mechanical, including photocopying, recording or by any
information storage and retrieval system, without written permission
from the copyright holder, except for a book review.

FAIRIES 3
Line Art Coloring book by Christine Karron
First published November 2019

ISBN: 9781710049725
Imprint: Independently published

Copyright 2019 Christine Karron
All rights reserved

www.chkarron.com

FAIRIES 3

1. Fairy Dance
2. Apple Tree Fairy
3. Moonchild Fae
4. Soulmates
5. Fairy Girl With Birds
6. Fairy Sleep
7. Lilac Fairy
8. New Islands Fairy
9. Bird Nest Fairy
10. Old Tree Fairy
11. Old Wise Fairy
12. Hummingbird Fairy
13. Fawn Fairy
14. Toadstool Fairy
15. Fairy Grandmother With Granddaughter
16. Fairy With The Little Lizard
17. Faelight Keeper
18. The Magic Flute
19. Fairy Bride
20. Stolen Fae

Bonus

21. Autumn
22. Halloween Tea Party
23. Snow Day Skating
24. Steampunk Huntress

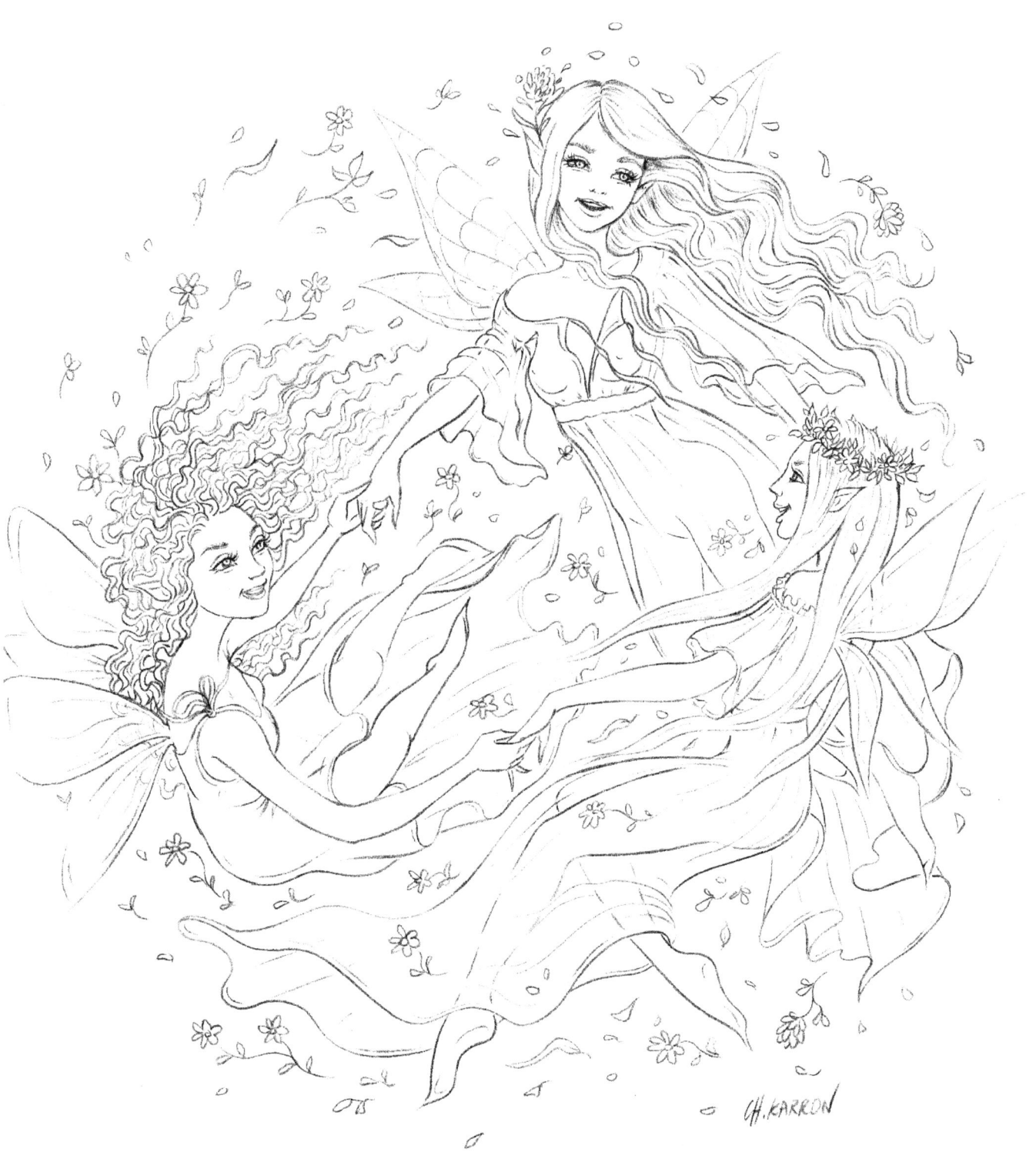

FAIRIES 3 Line Art by Christine Karron   Fairy Dance

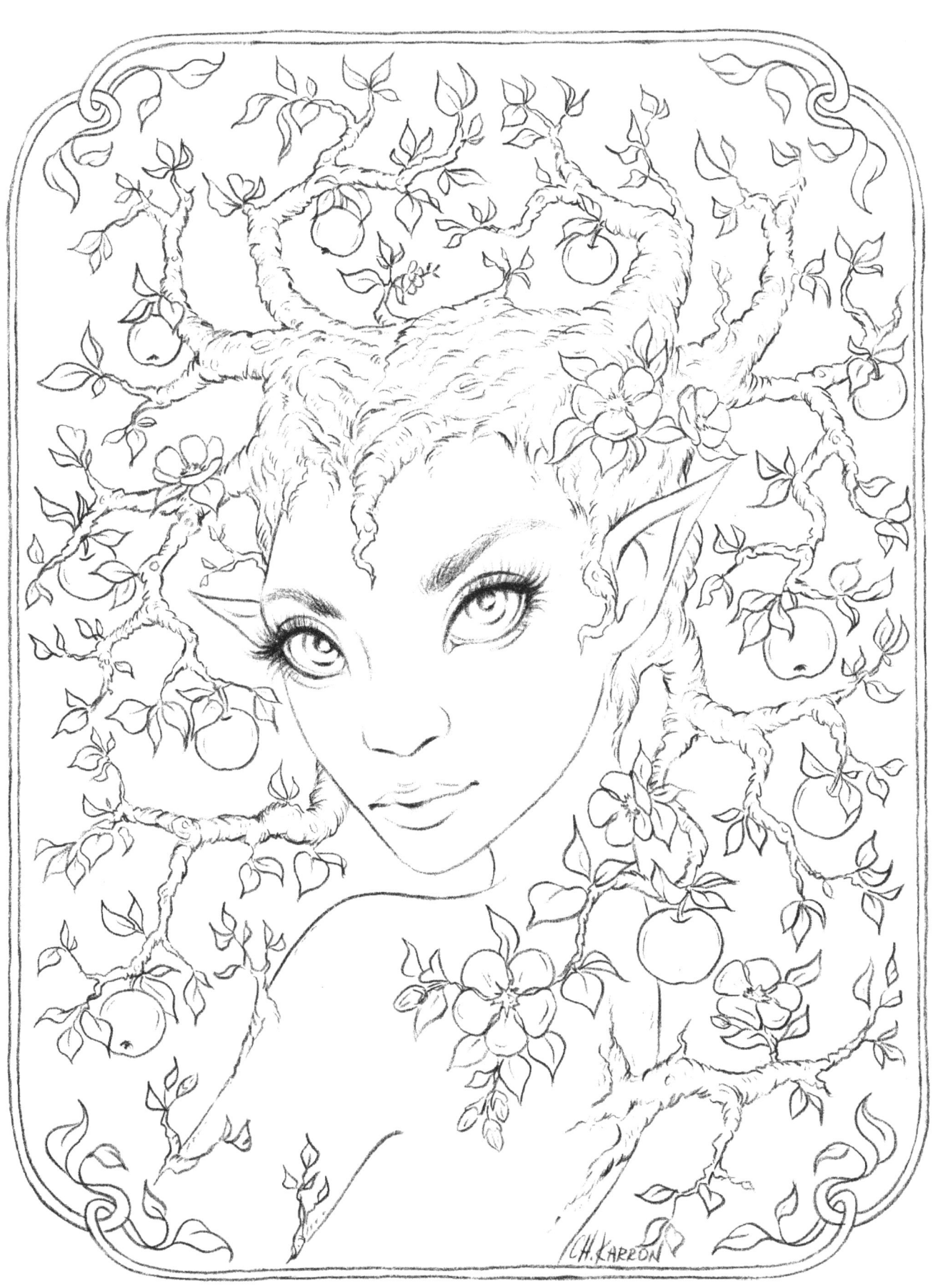

FAIRIES 3 Line Art by Christine Karron Apple Tree Fairy

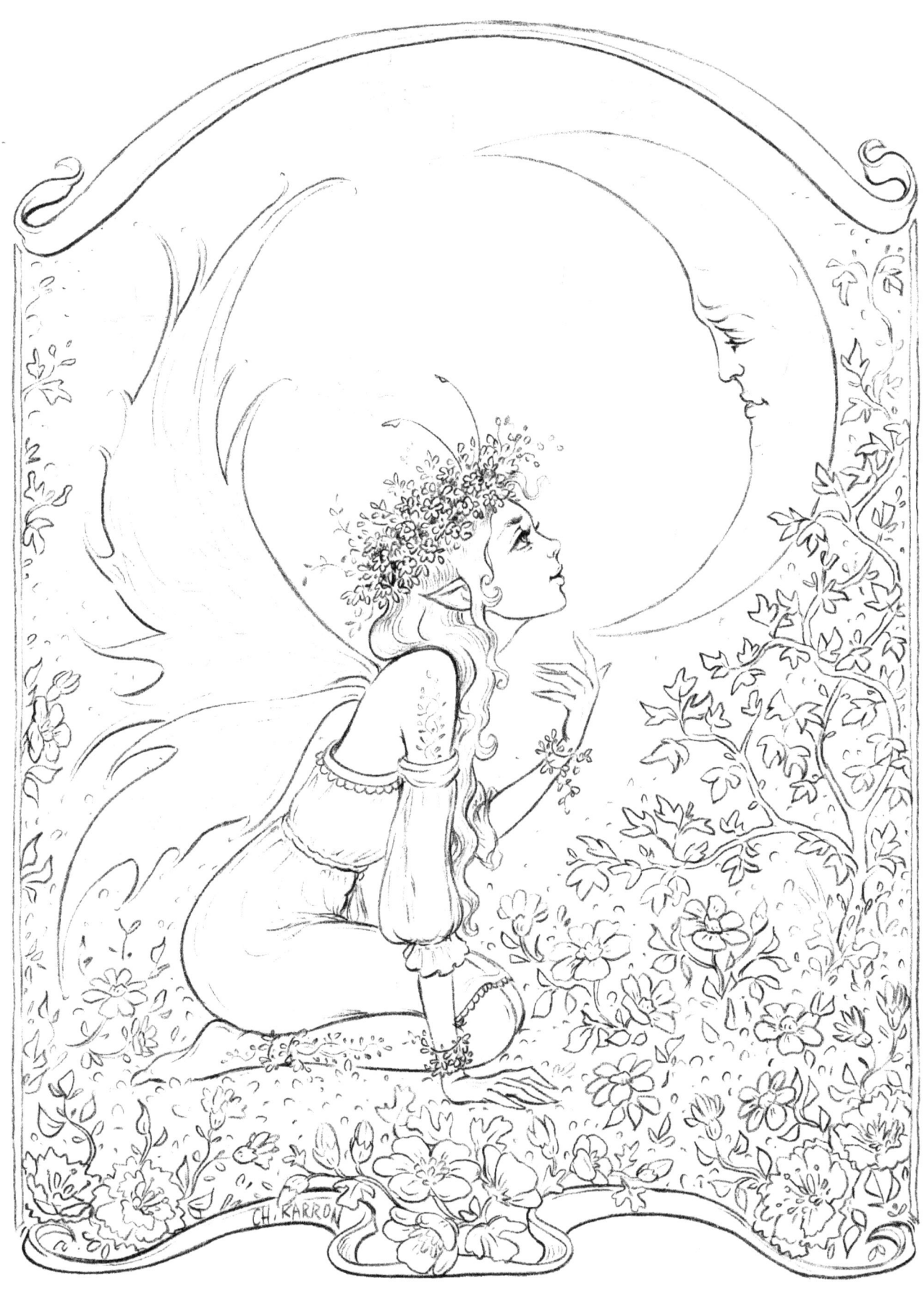

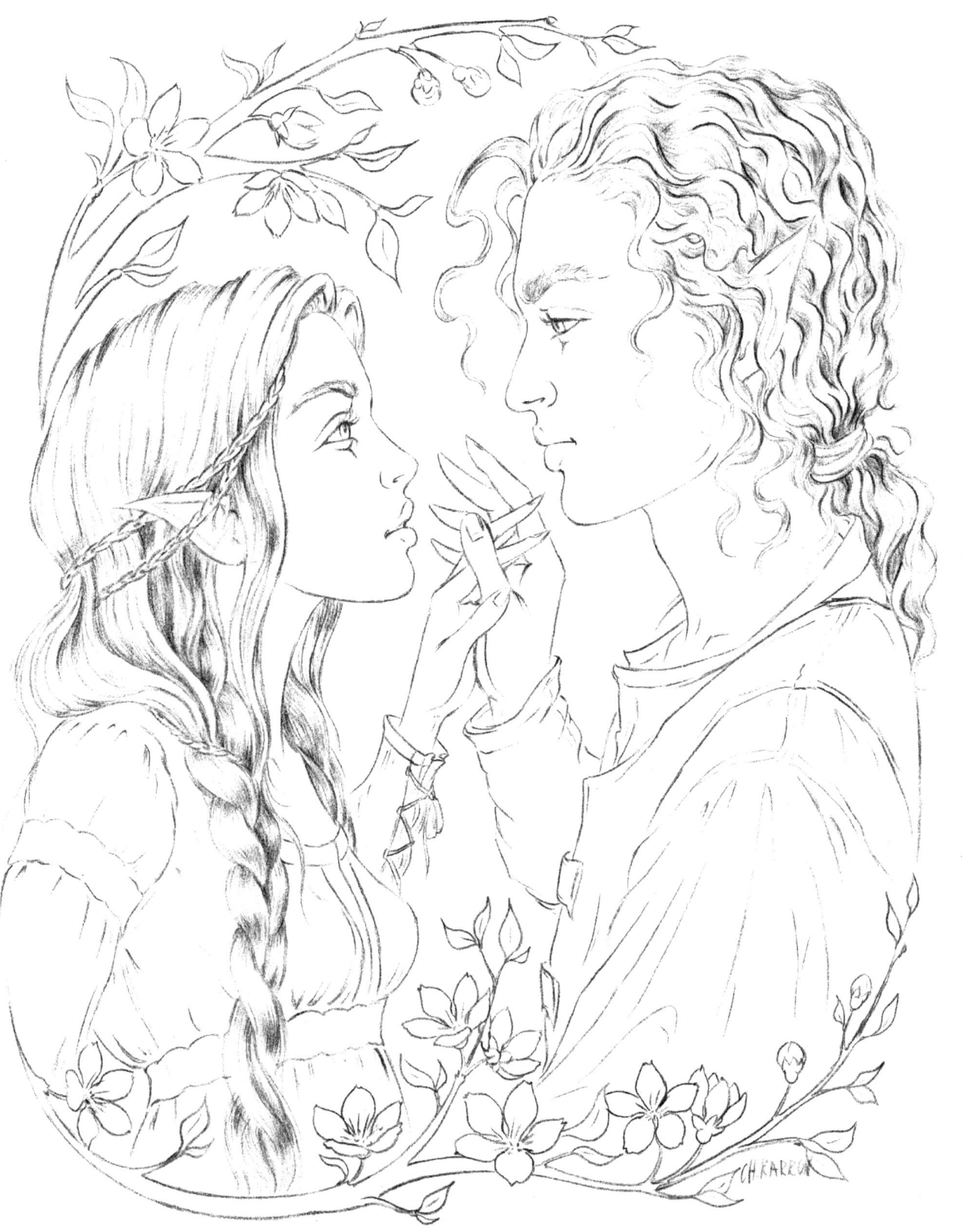

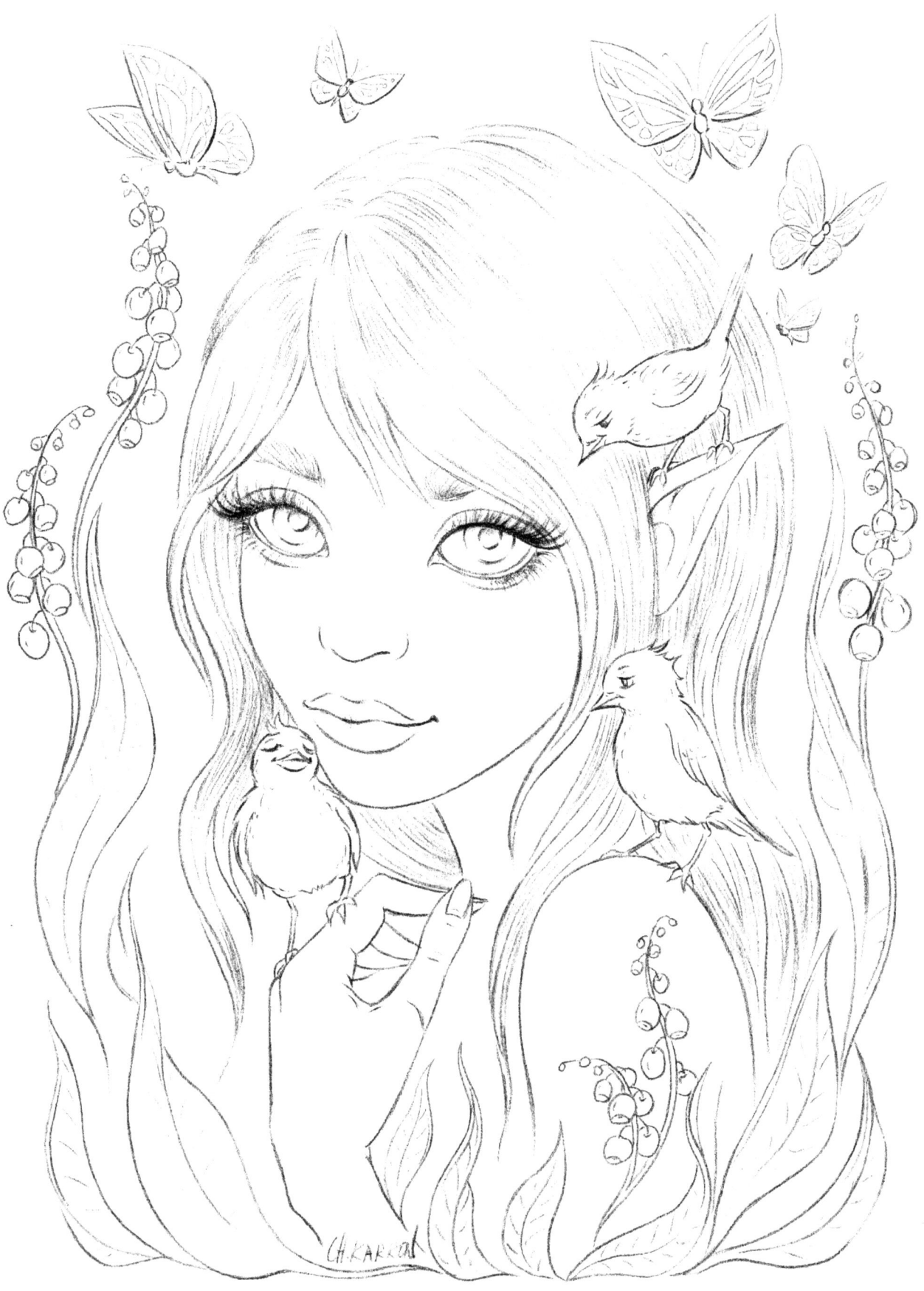

FAIRIES 3 Line Art by Christine Karron   Fairy Girl With Birds

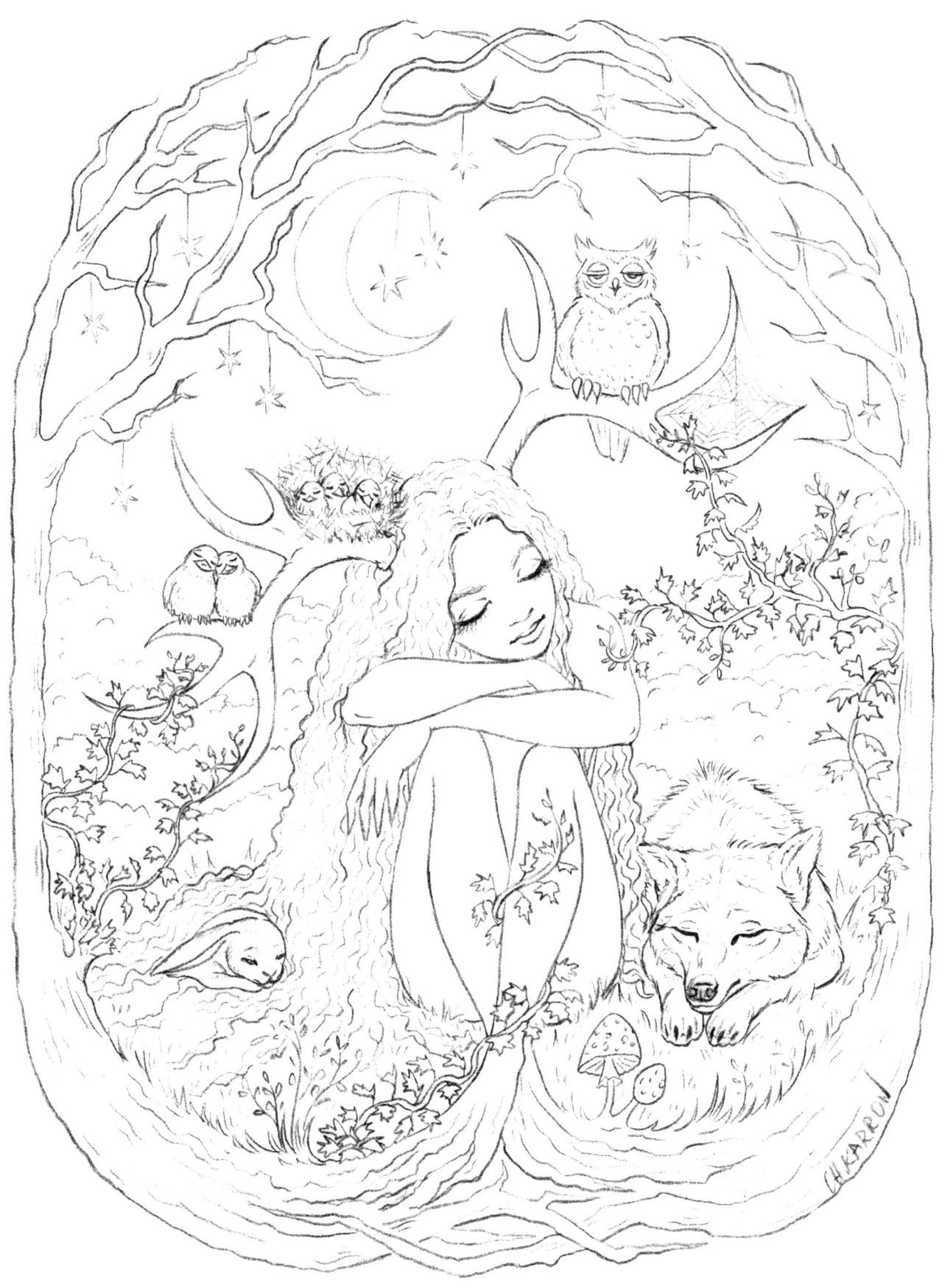

FAIRIES 3 Line Art by Christine Karron

Fairy Sleep

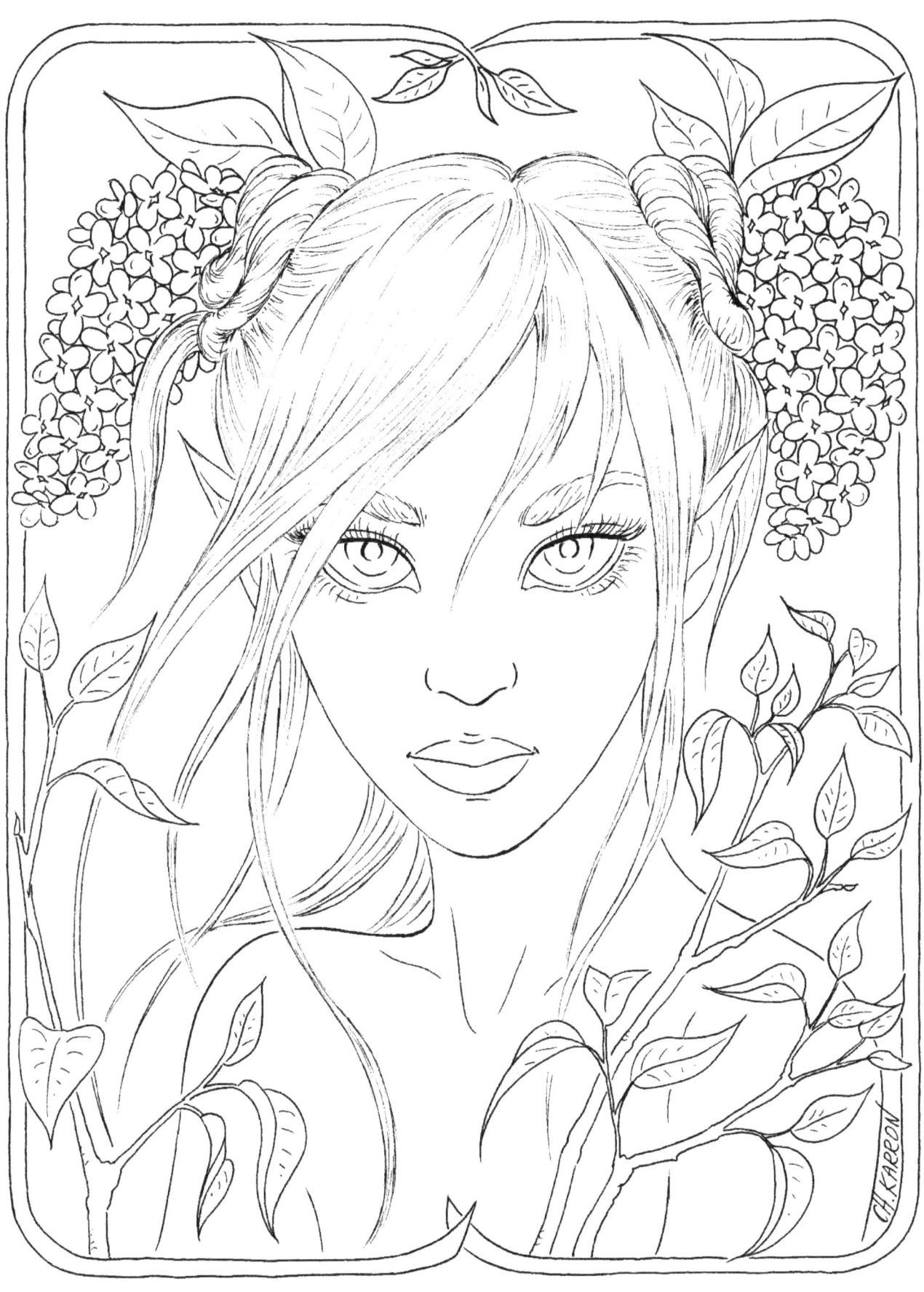

FAIRIES 3 *Line Art by Christine Karron* *Lilac Fairy*

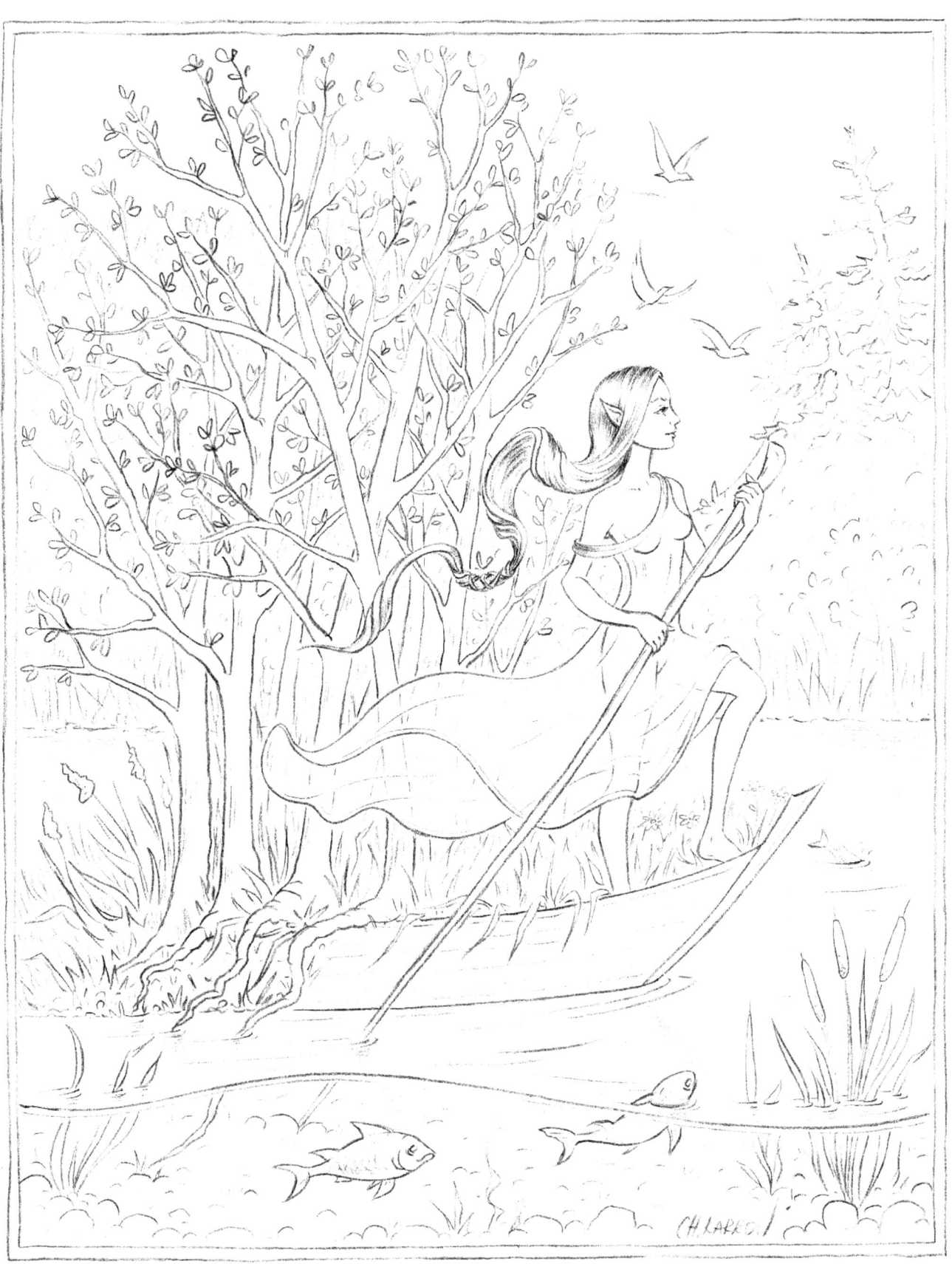

FAIRIES 3 Line Art by Christine Karron New Islands Fairy

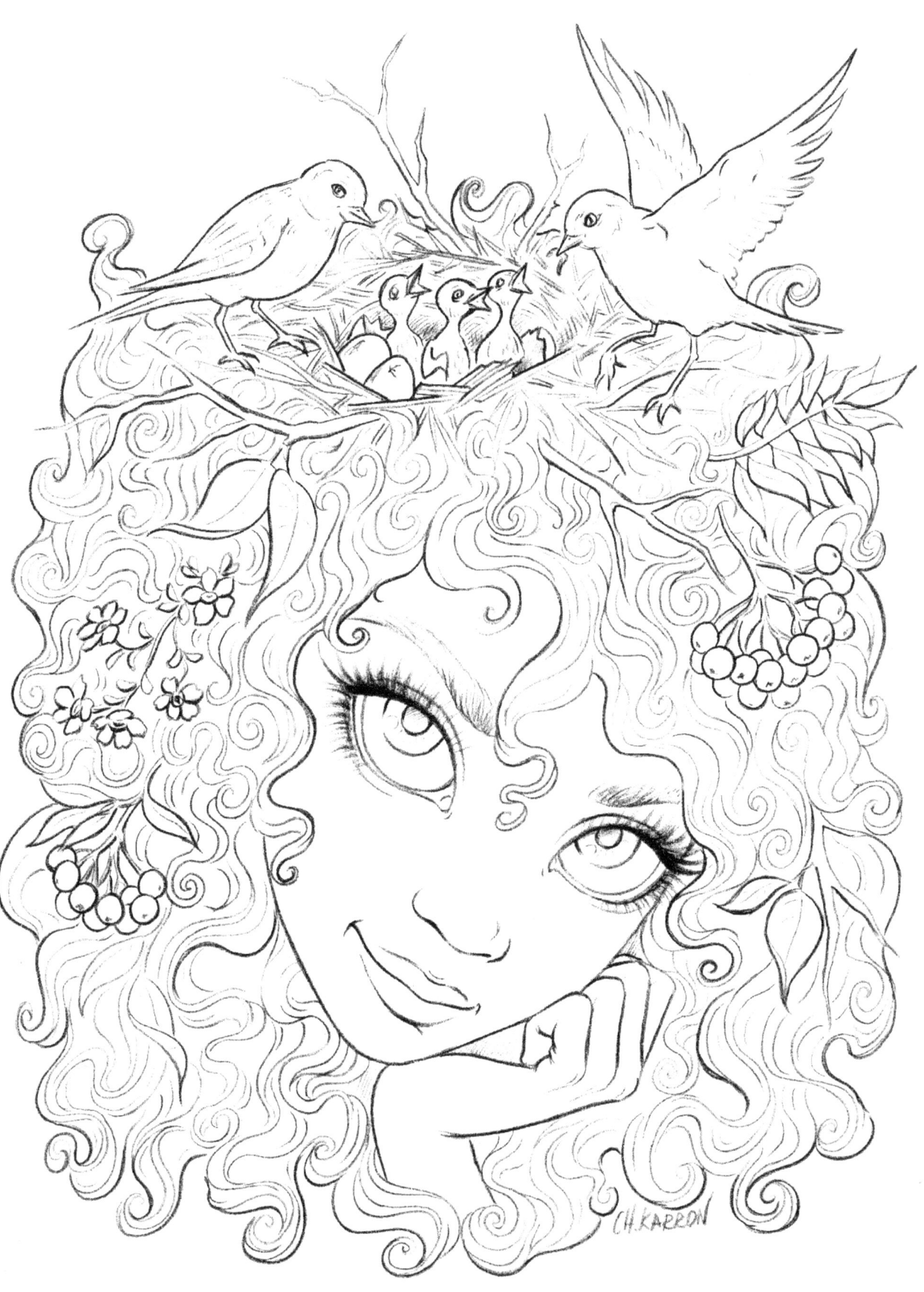

FAIRIES 3 *Line Art by Christine Karron* Bird Nest Fairy

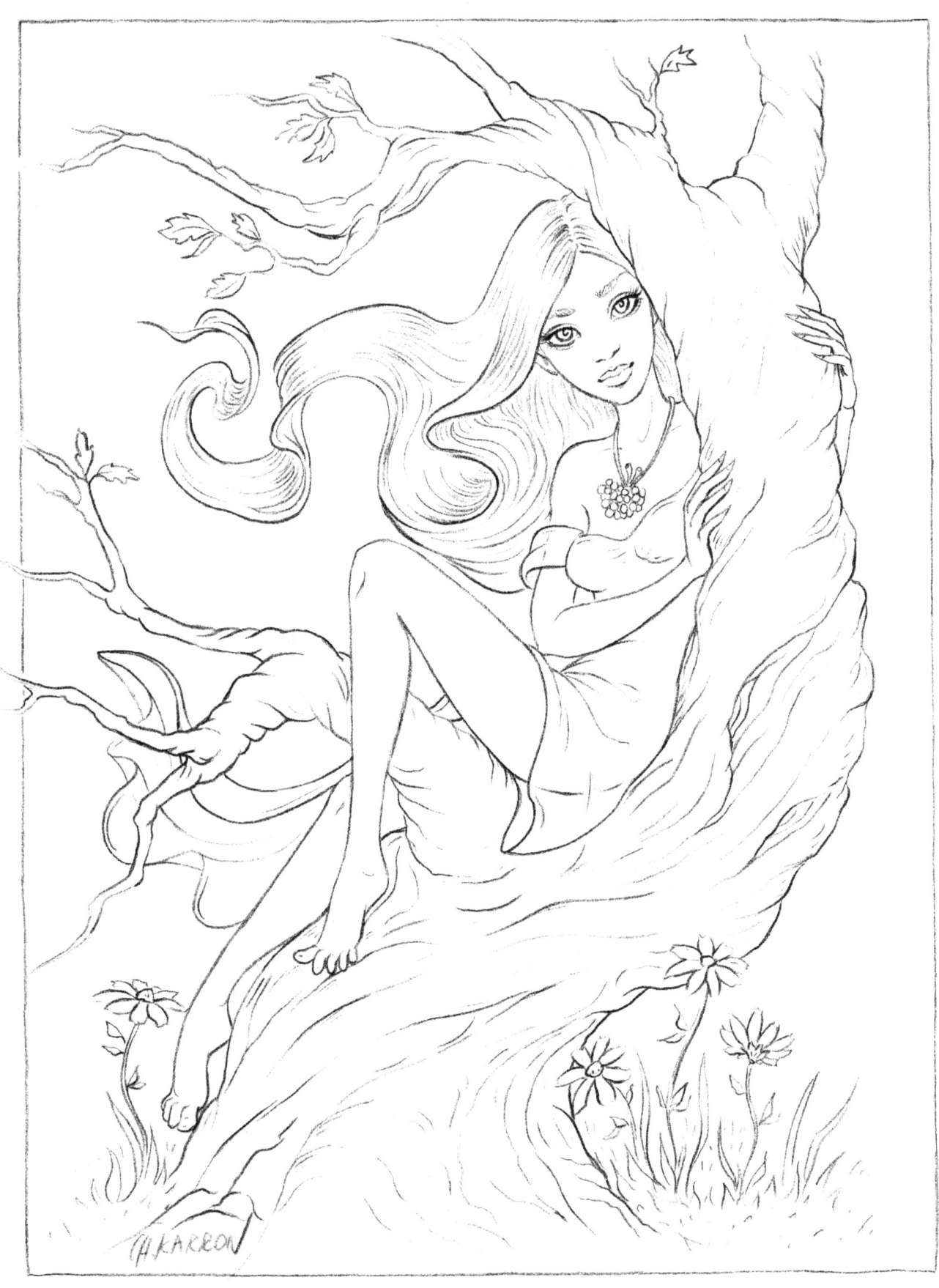

Fairies 3 Line Art by Christine Karron — *Old Tree Fairy*

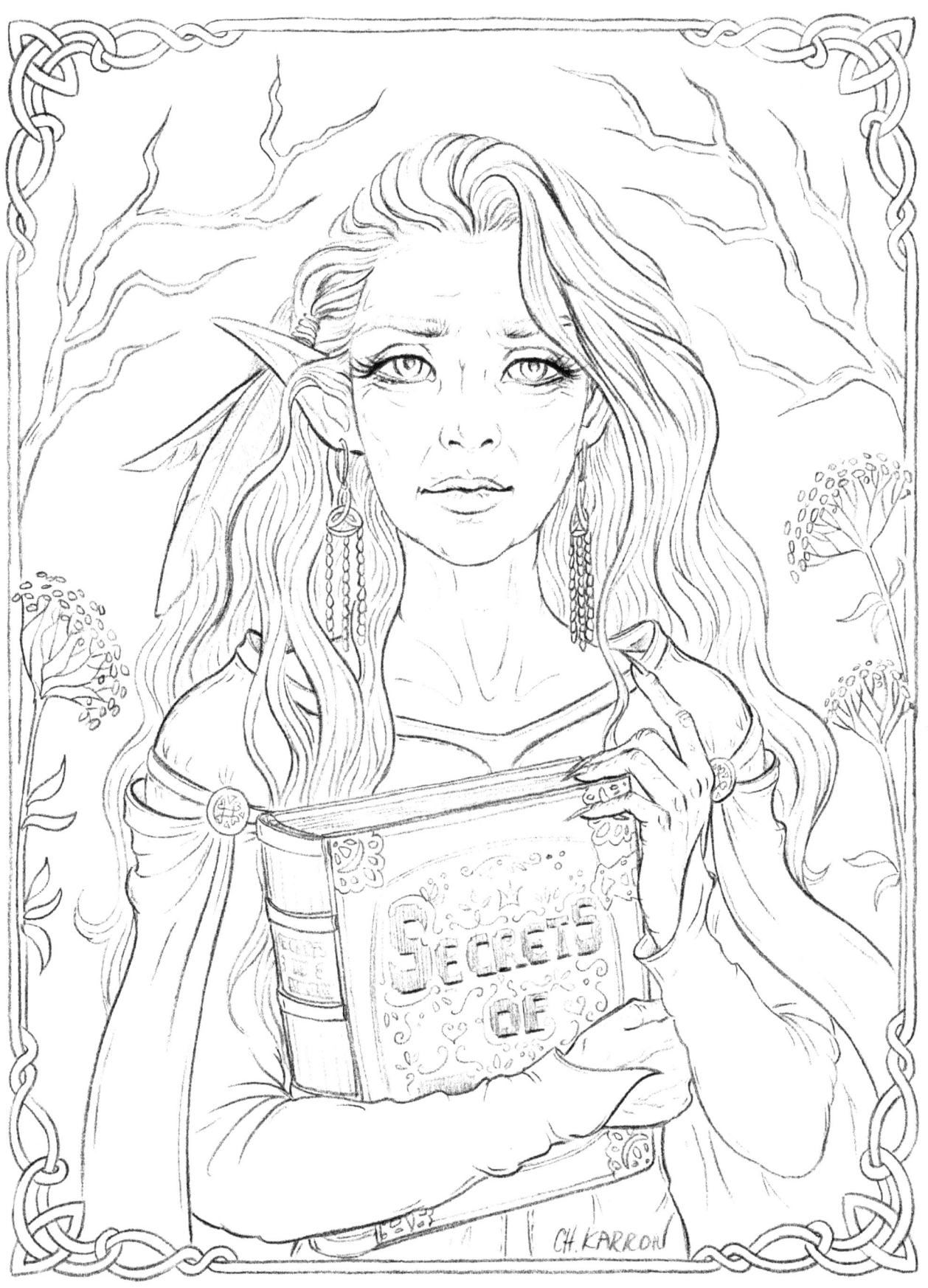

FAIRIES 3 *Line Art by Christine Karron* *Old Wise Fairy*

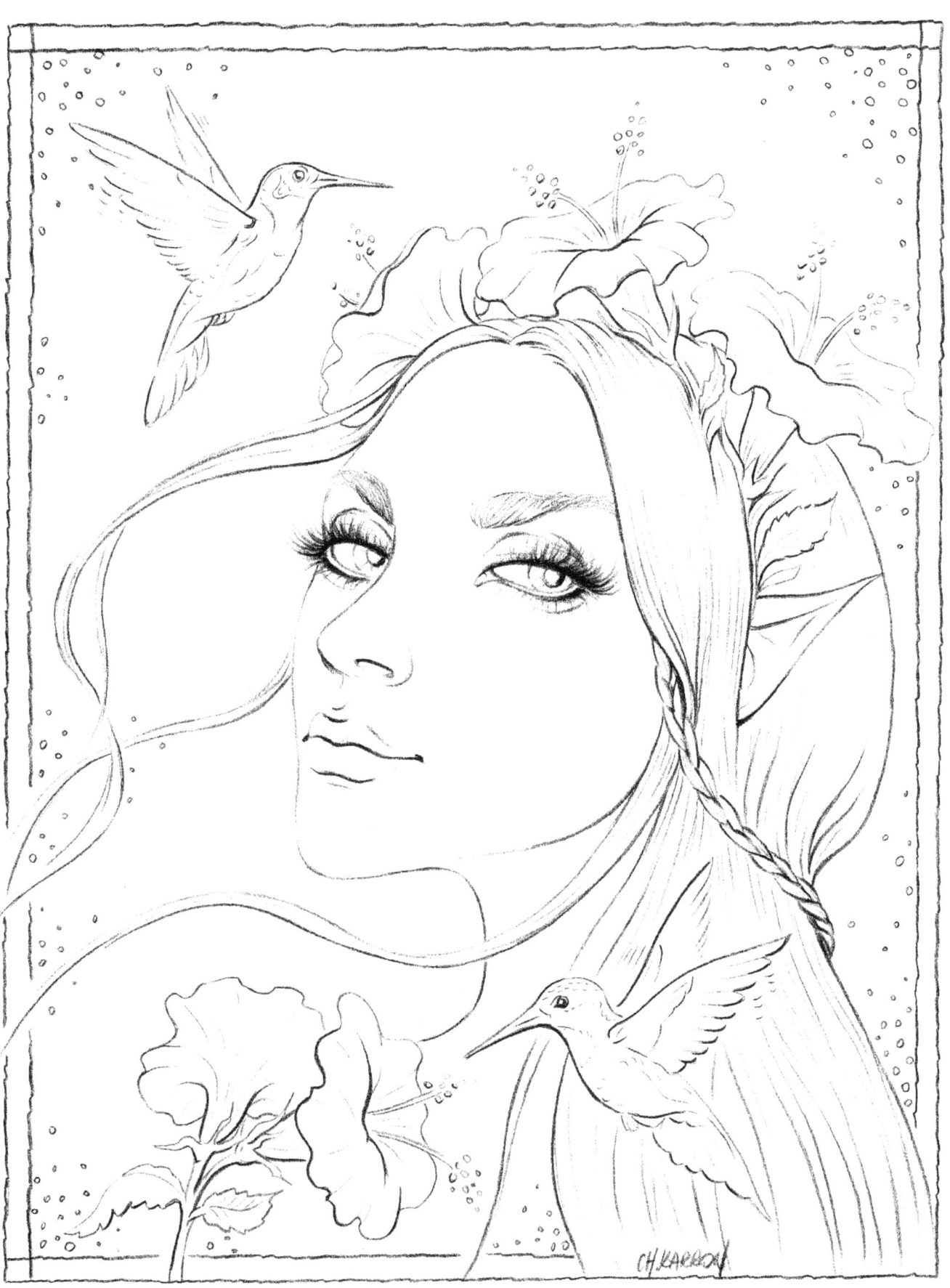

FAIRIES 3 Line Art by Christine Karron — Hummingbird Fairy

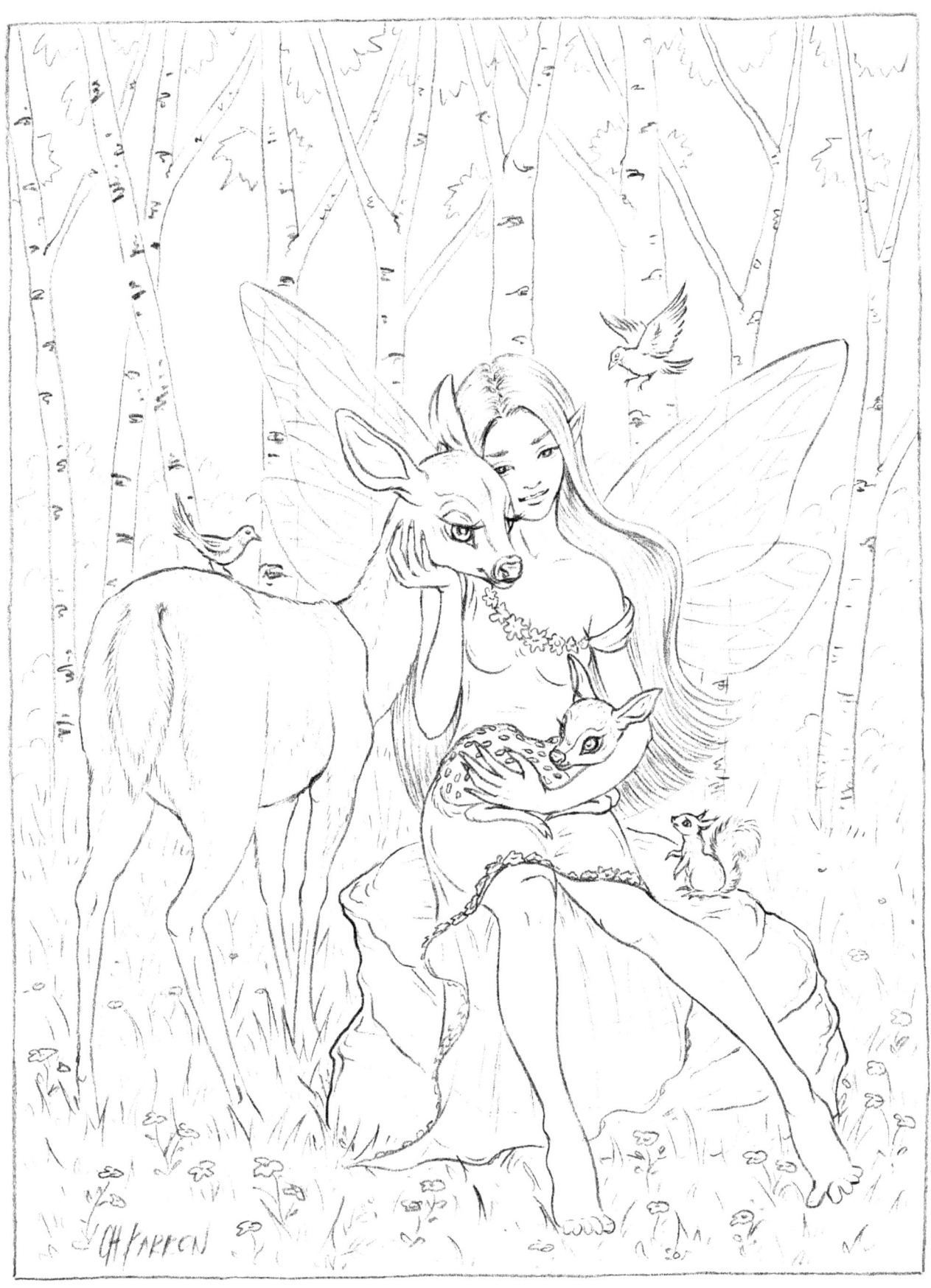

FAIRIES 3 Line Art by Christine Karron Fawn Fairy

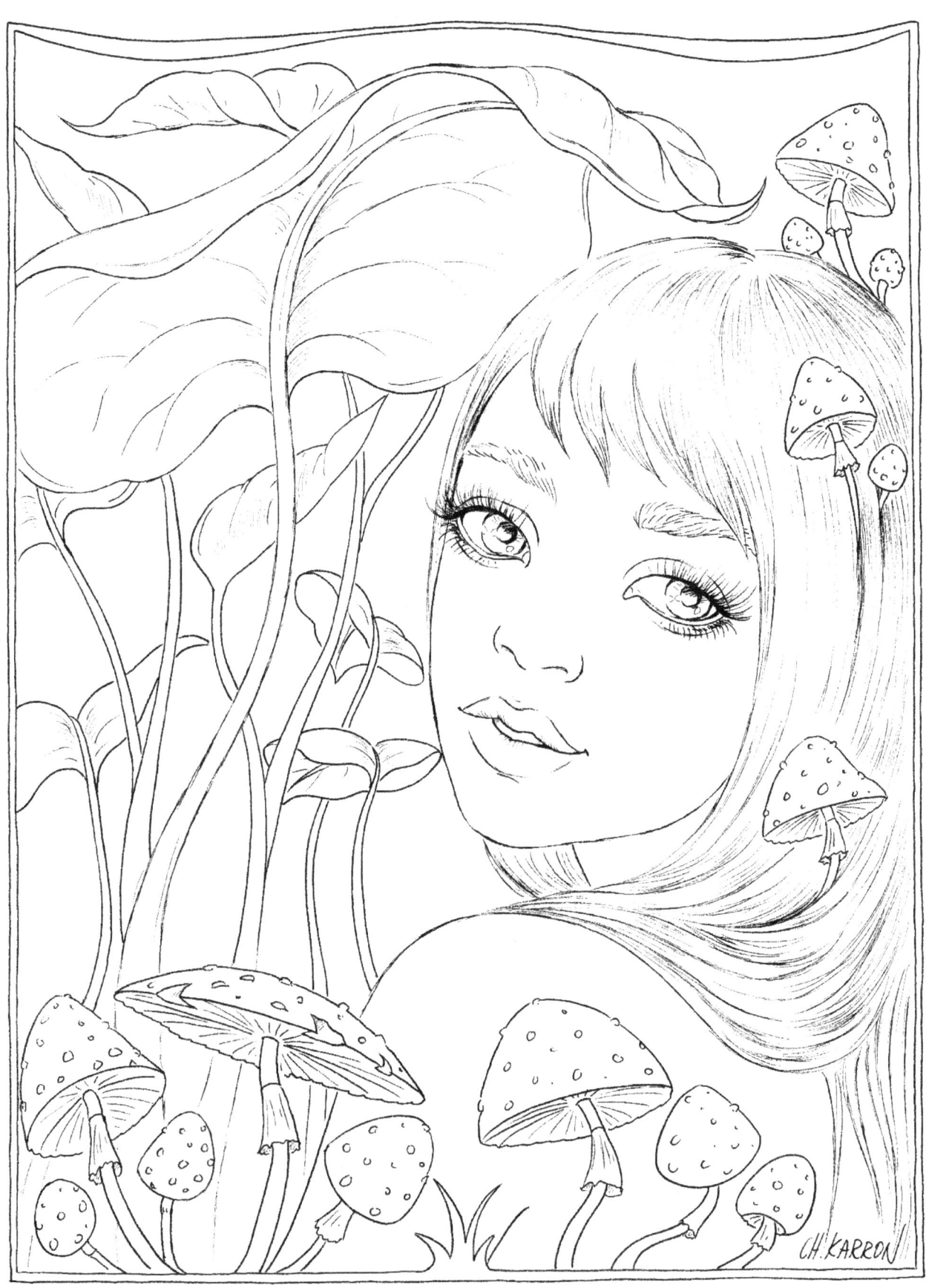

FAIRIES 3 Line Art by Christine Karron Toadstool Fairy

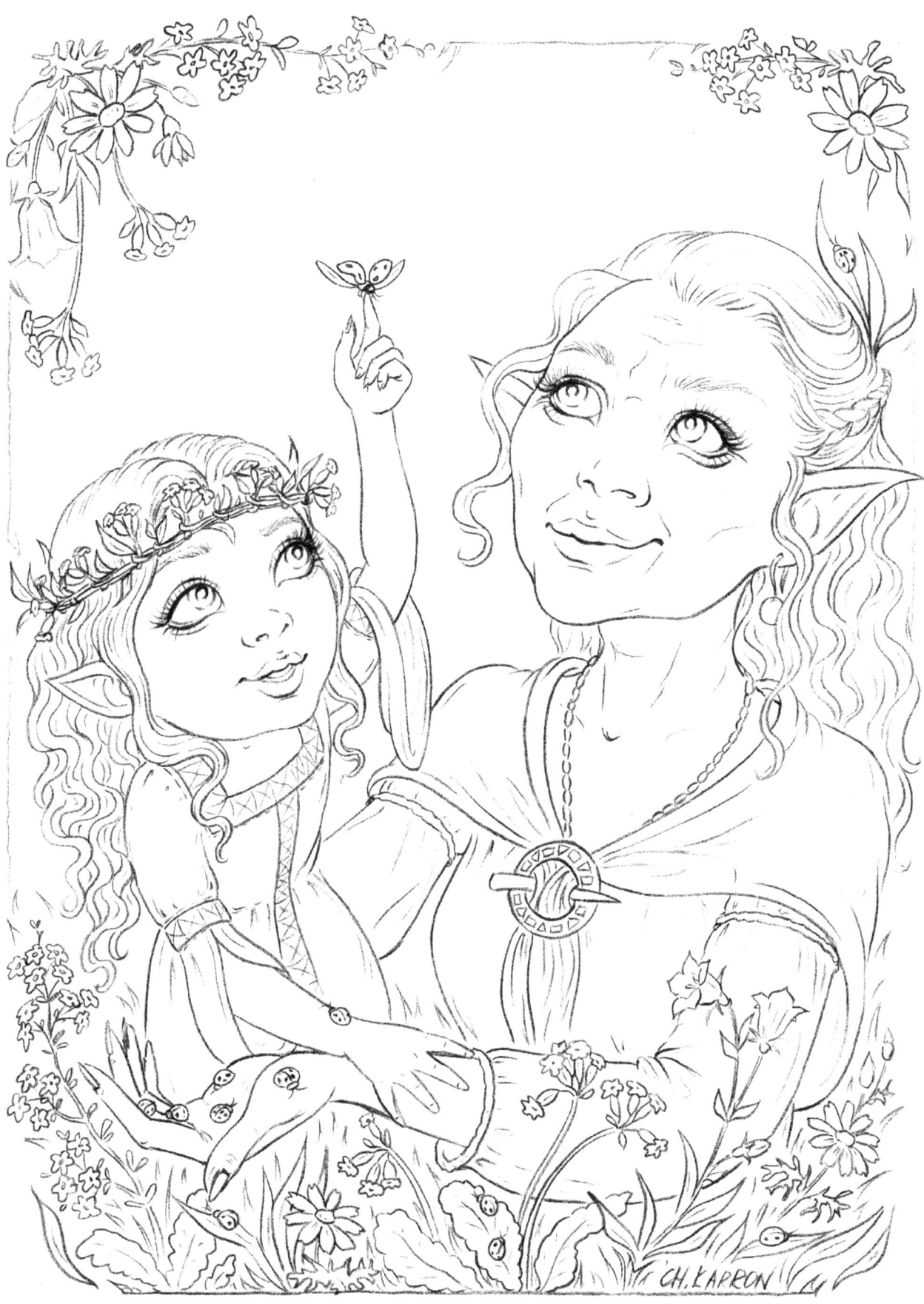

FAIRIES 3 Line Art by Christine Karron — Fairy Grandmother With Granddaughter

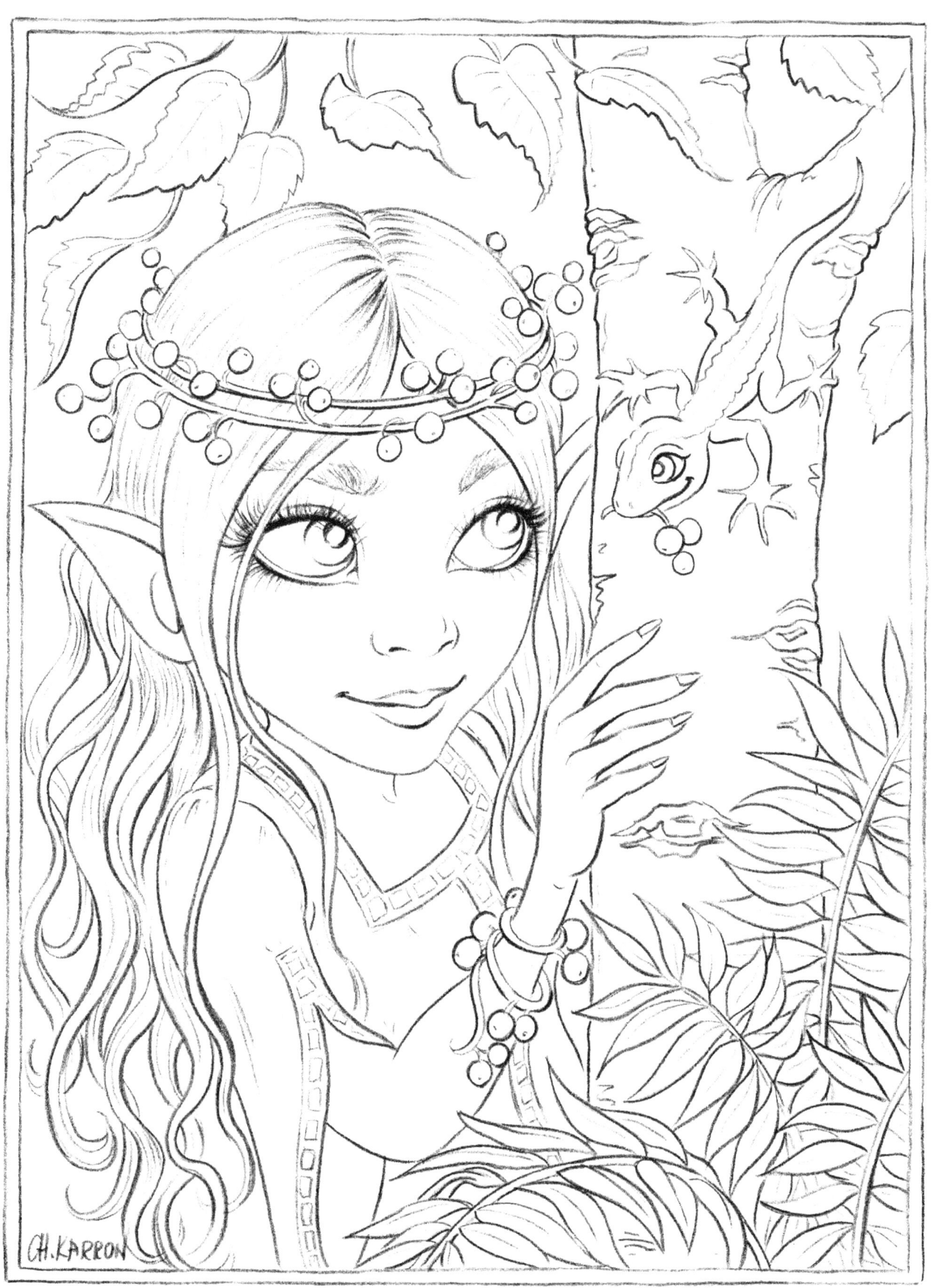

FAIRIES 3 *Line Art by Christine Karron* *Fairy With The Little Lizard*

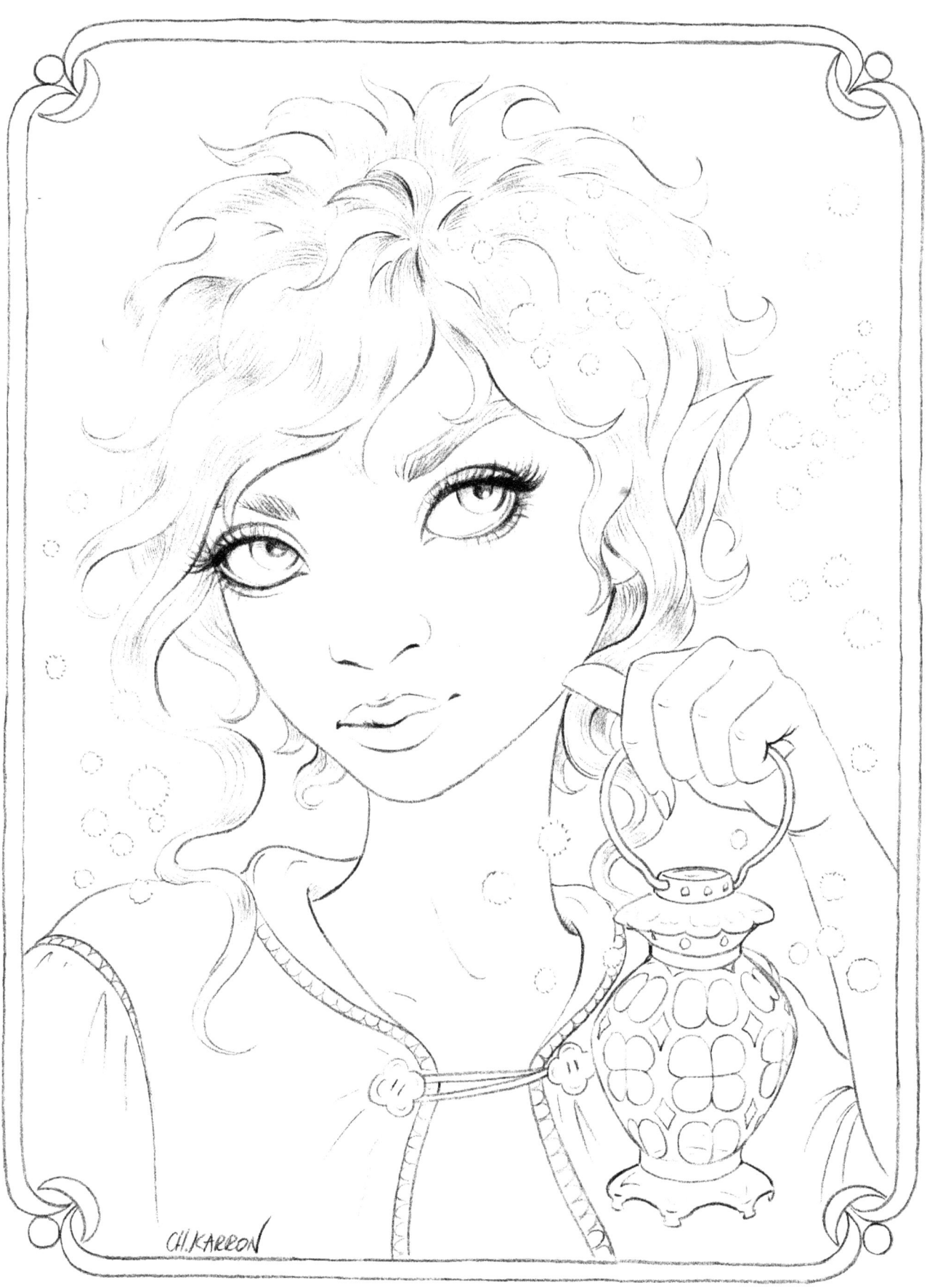

FAIRIES 3 Line Art by Christine KarronFaelight Keeper

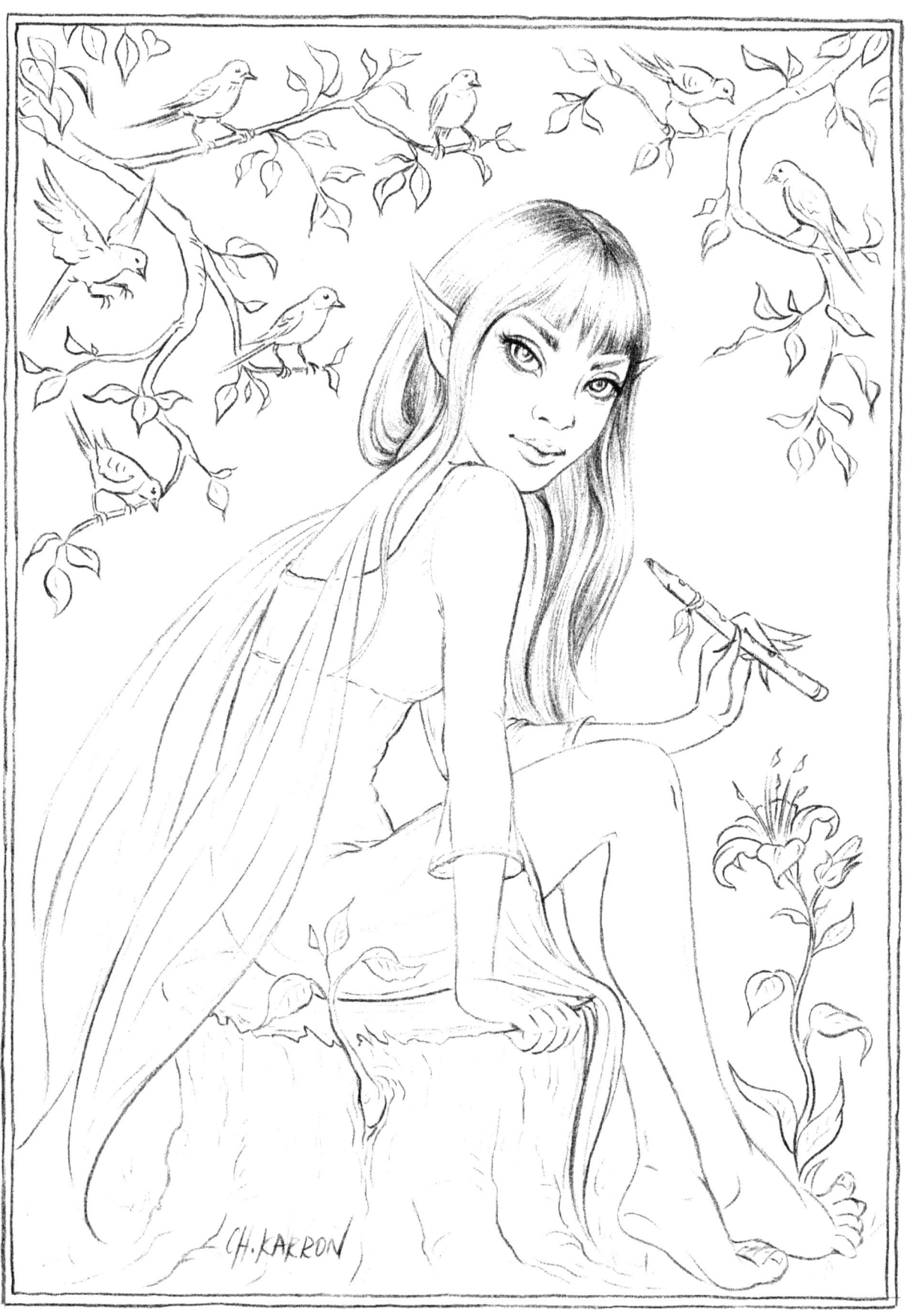

FAIRIES 3 Line Art by Christine Karron　　　　The Magic Flute

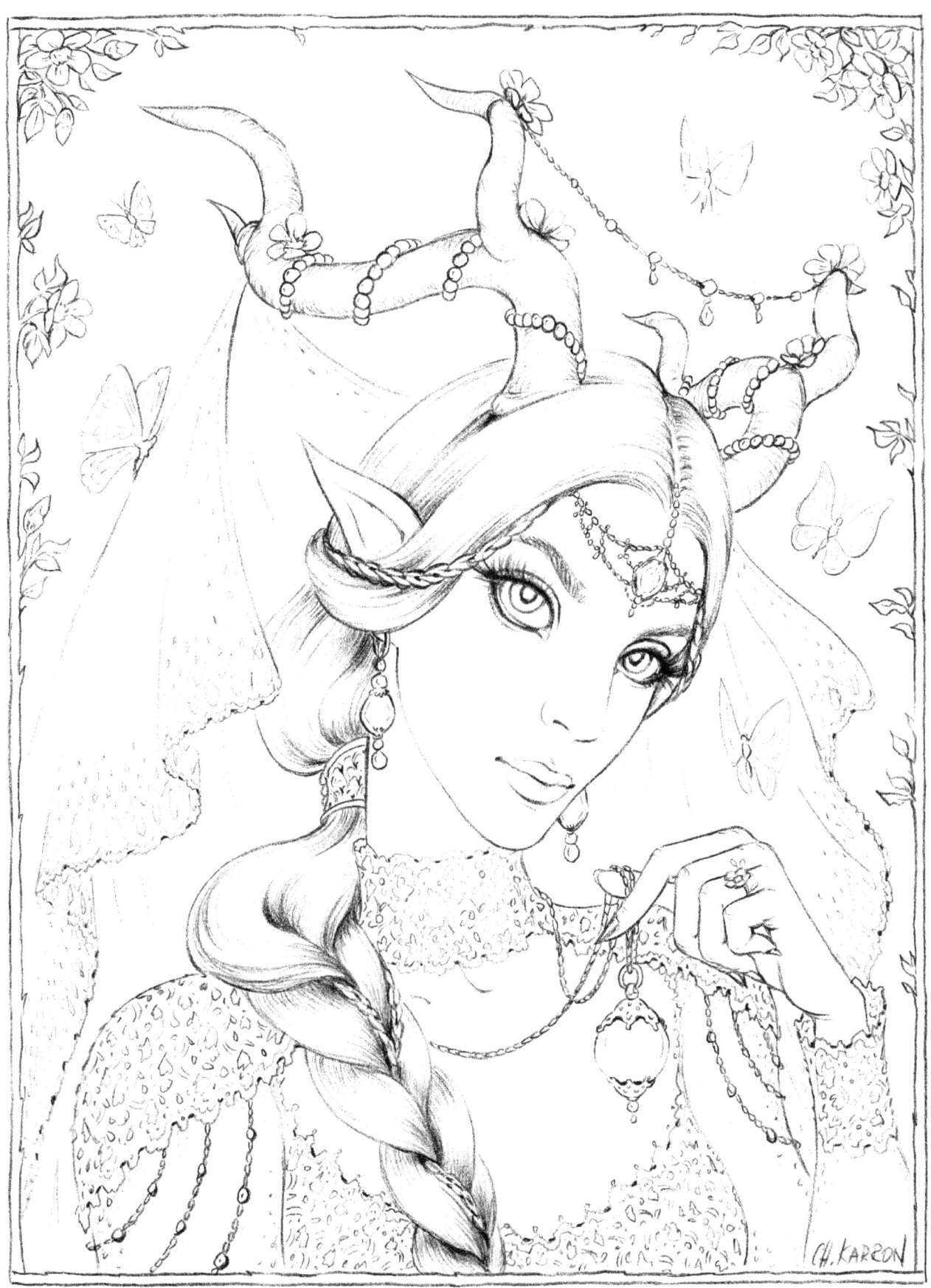

FAIRIES 3 Line Art by Christine Karron

Fairy Bride

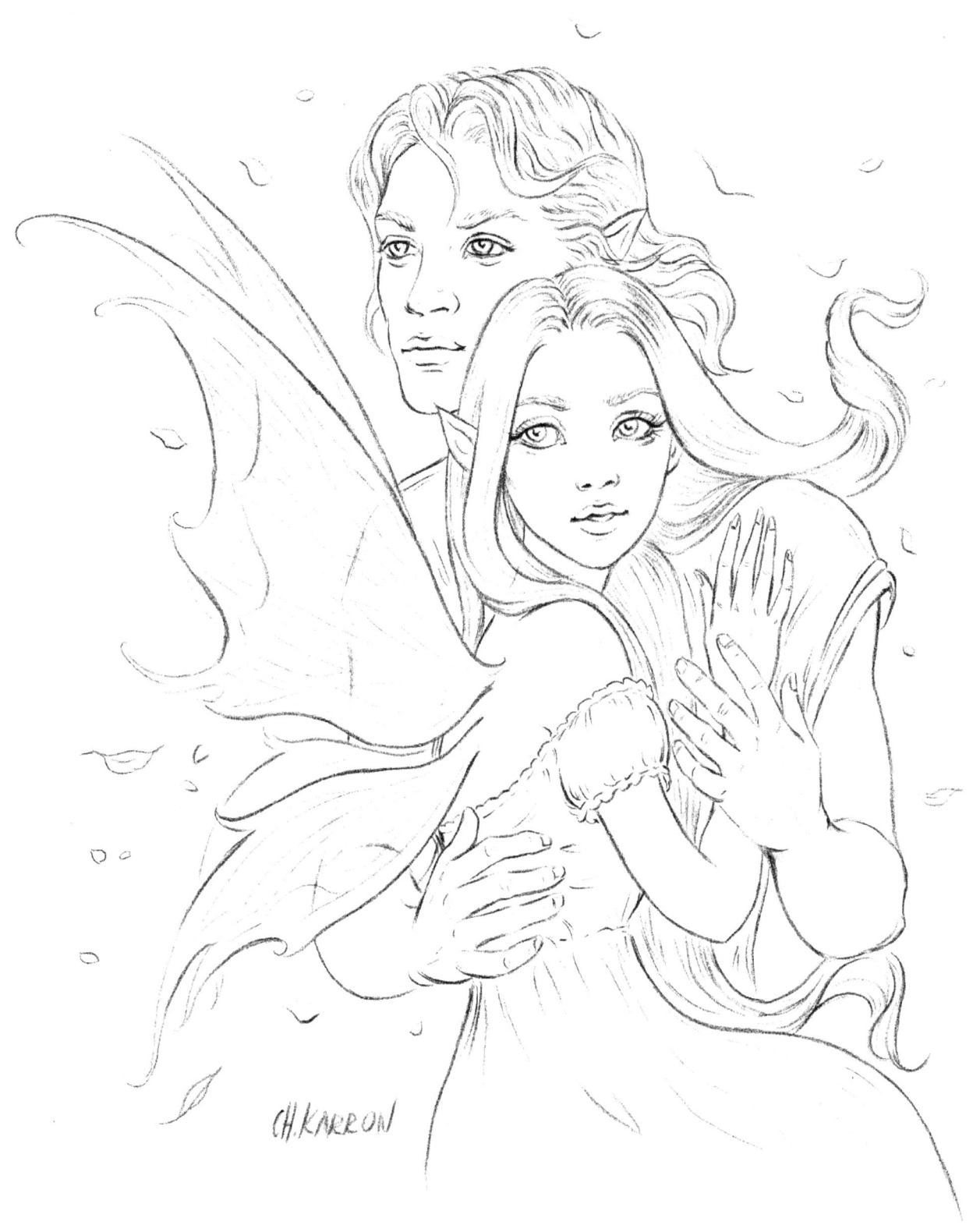

FAIRIES 3 *Line Art by Christine Karron* — Stolen Fae

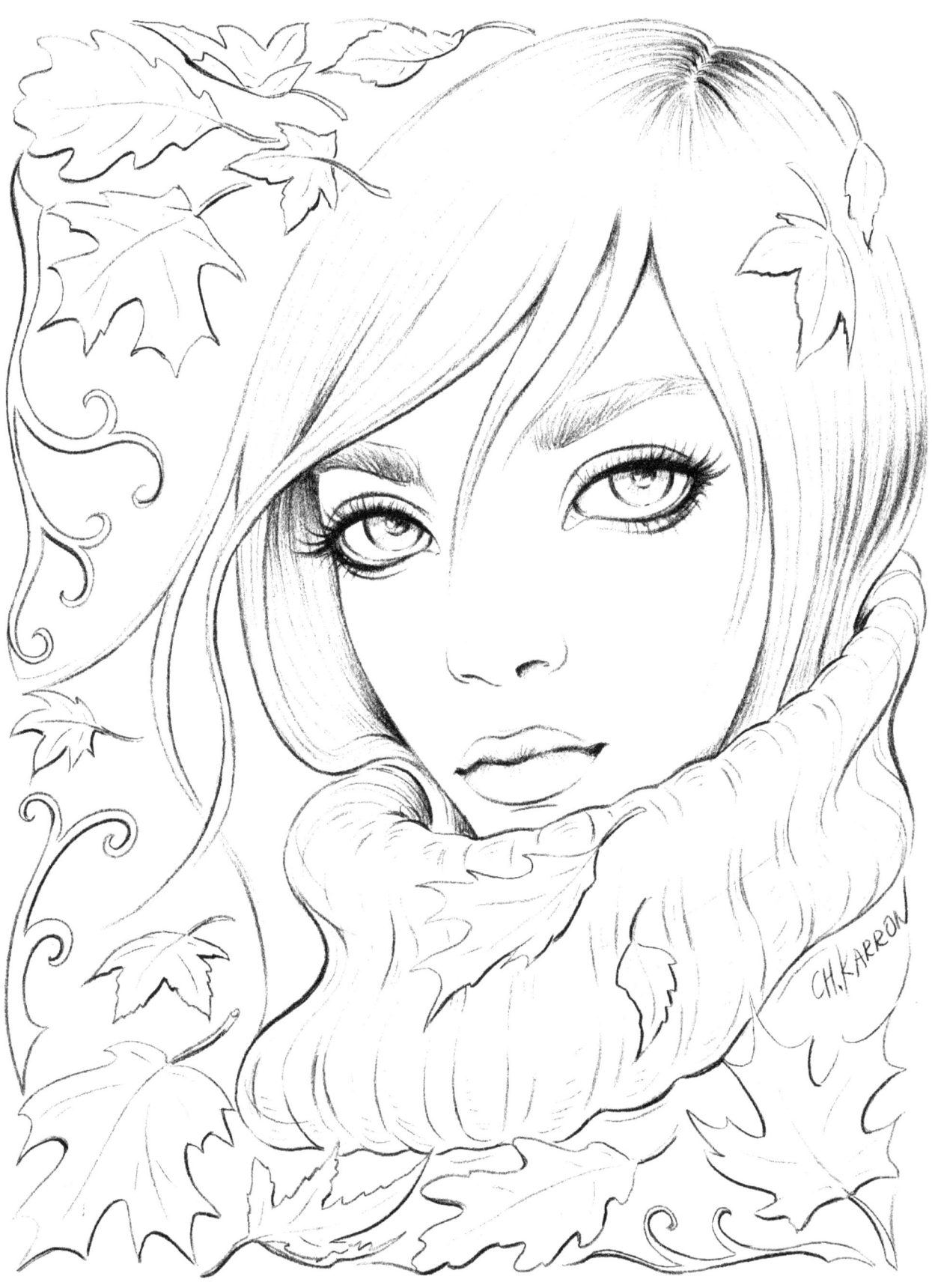

FAIRIES 3 Line Art by Christine Karron   Autumn

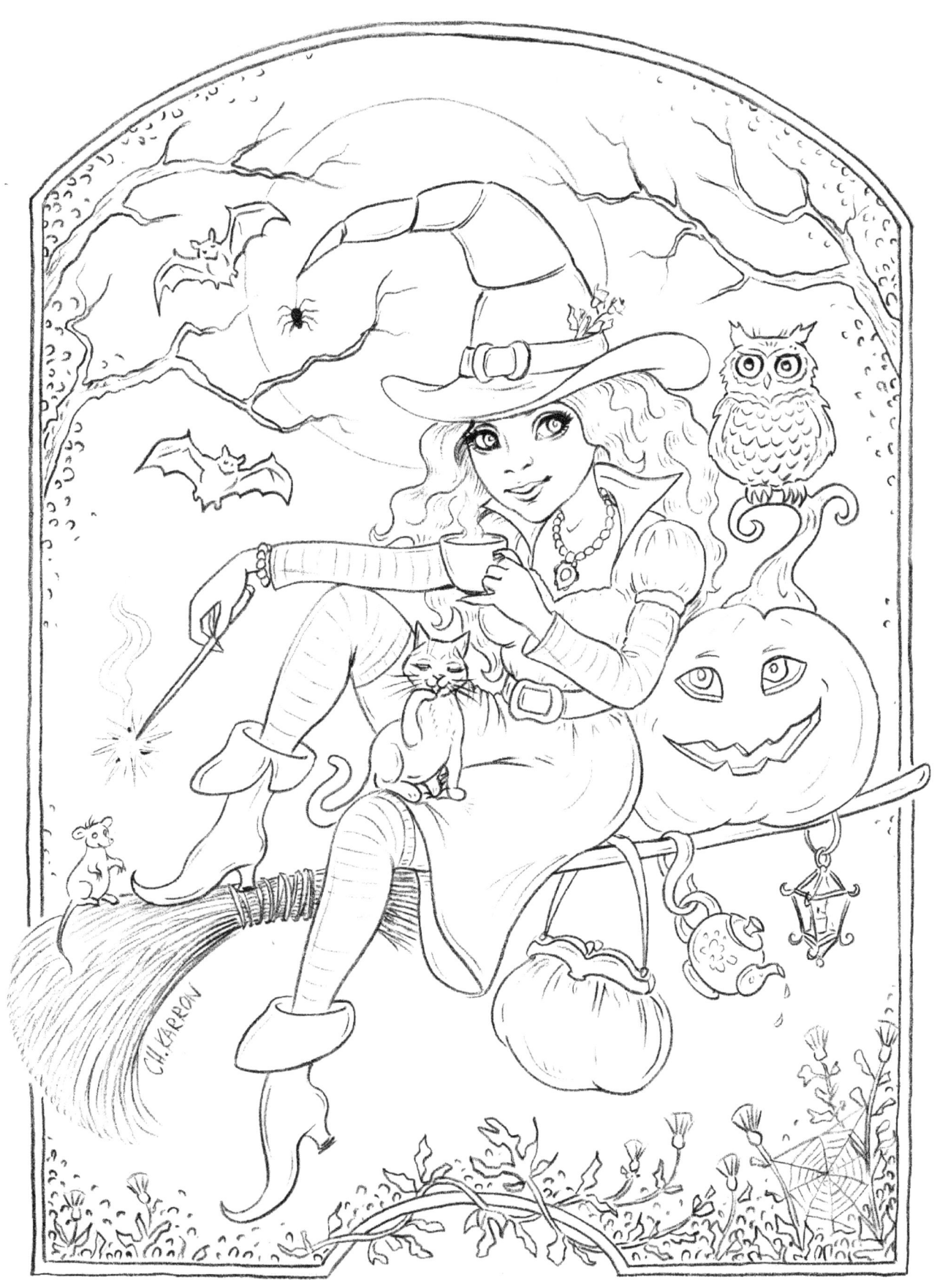

FAIRIES 3 Line Art by Christine Karron — Halloween Tea Party

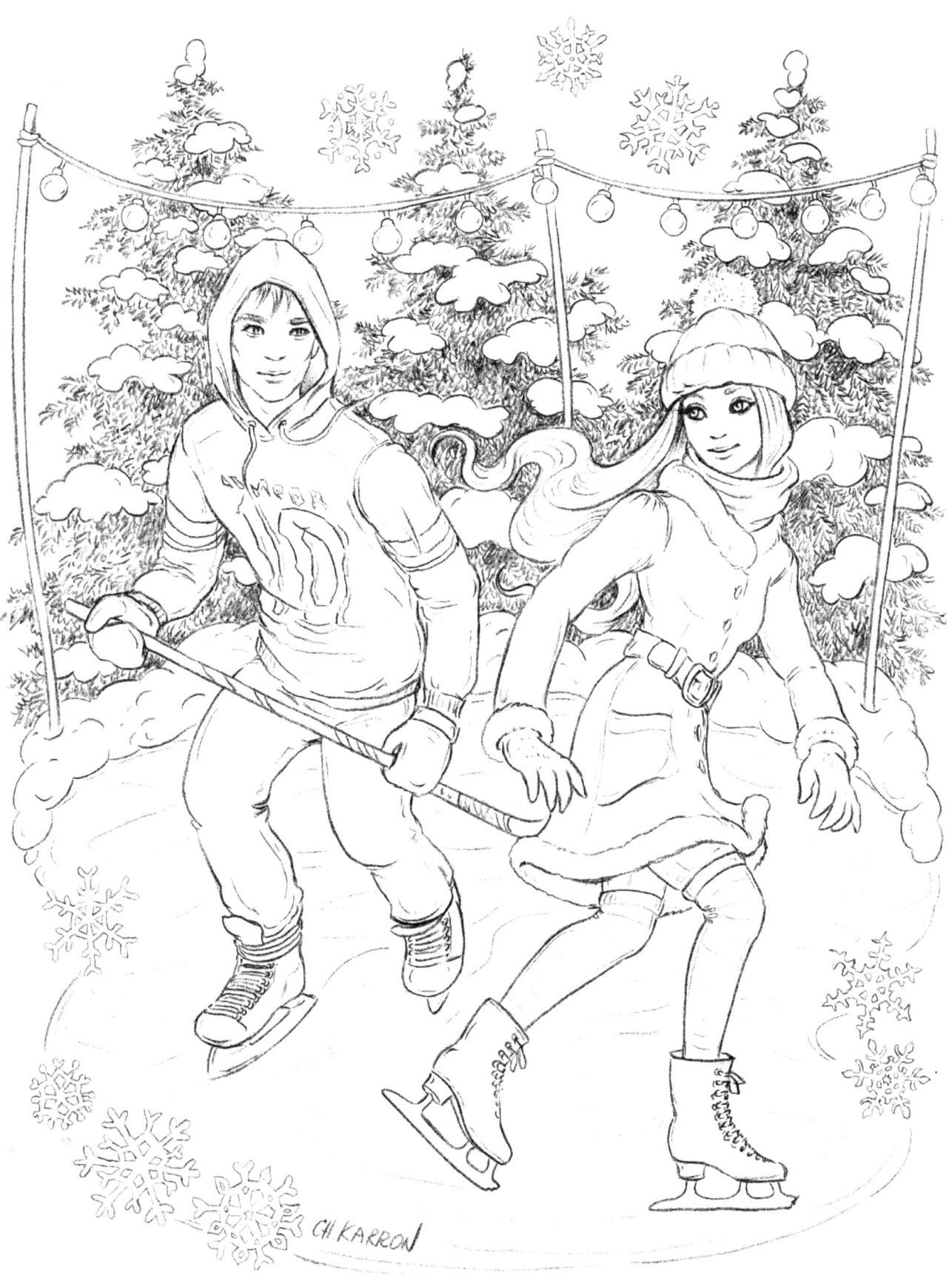

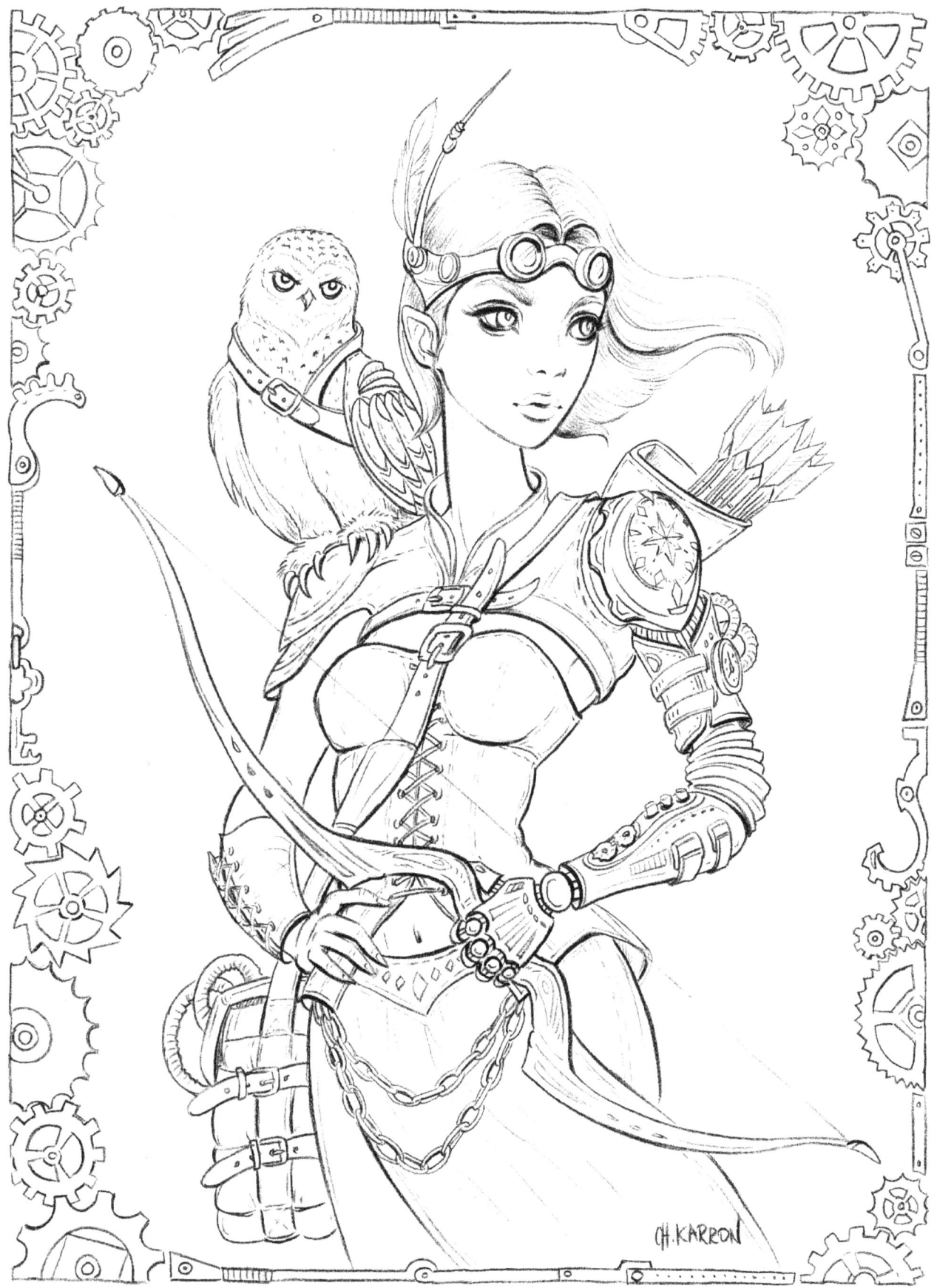

FAIRIES 3 *Line Art by Christine Karron* — *Steampunk Huntress*

Also available:

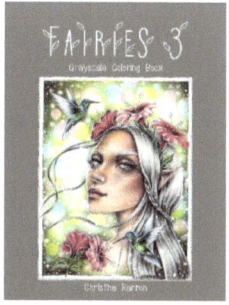 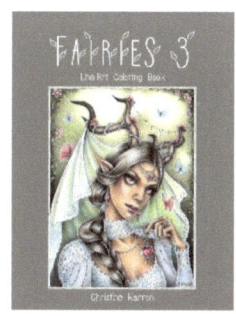 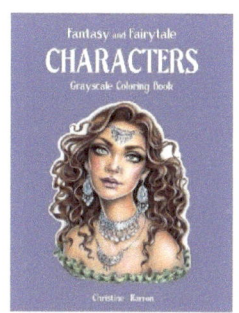 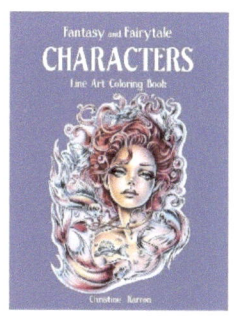 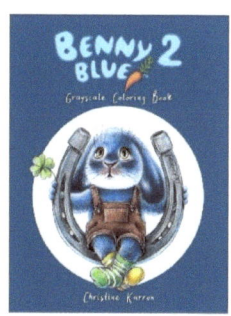

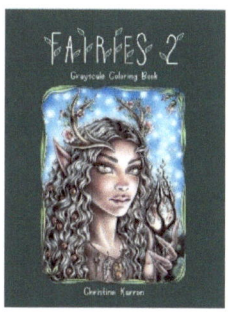 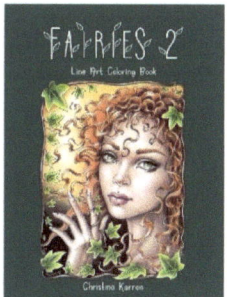 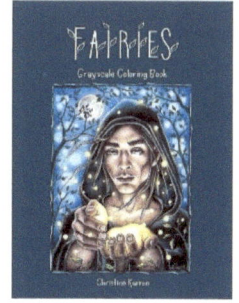 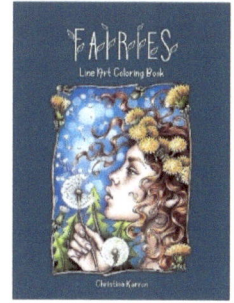 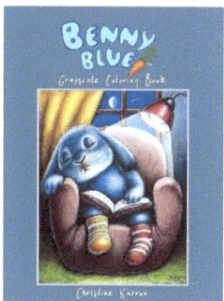

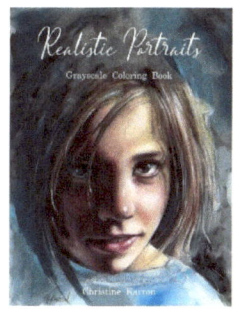 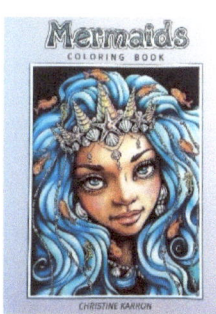 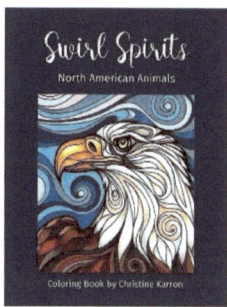

***

*Christine Karron is an artist and illustrator based in Alberta, Canada.
Drawing and painting has always been Christine's passion.
With some formal training, self-education and experience,
between raising kids and taking care of her family,
Christine has been working as a freelance artist for over 20 years.*

*Christine has illustrated 6 children's books and a few years ago
she started the adventure of self-publishing coloring books.
Christine loves to create fantasy illustrations and characters
with a whimsical, narrative and humorous touch.
Working traditionally, she uses primarily colored pencils,
ink pens/markers and watercolor on paper.*

You can follow Christine Karron on Facebook, Instagram and Twitter.

Printable digital downloads (in PDF format) of coloring books and
single coloring pages are available in Christine Karron's Etsy shop.

Join Christine's Patreon page for a monthly coloring page.

You are welcome to join Christine Karron
Coloring Collection Fan Group on Facebook.

Visit www.chkarron.com for coloring ideas and samples,
or watch demo videos on Christine's Youtube channel.

If sharing colored images online please credit the artist - Christine Karron
You can use hashtags #christinekarron and/or #chkarron
Please DO NOT share or post uncolored versions of the images from this book
on Facebook, Pinterest or any other sharing sites online.

All rights reserved by Christine Karron
www.chkarron.com

www.ingramcontent.com/pod-product-compliance
Lightning Source LLC
Chambersburg PA
CBHW051214220526
45473CB00003B/1027